LOVE IS
A PLACE

BUT YOU CANNOT LIVE THERE

FIRST POETS SERIES 23

Guernica Editions Inc. acknowledges the support of
the Canada Council for the Arts and the Ontario Arts Council.
The Ontario Arts Council is an agency of the Government of Ontario.
We acknowledge the financial support of the Government of Canada

◎◎◎ Jade Wallace ◎◎◎

LOVE IS A PLACE

BUT YOU CANNOT LIVE THERE

GUERNICA
EDITIONS

TORONTO • CHICAGO • BUFFALO • LANCASTER (U.K.)
2023

Guernica Founder: Antonio D'Alfonso

Michael Mirolla, general editor
Elana Wolff, editor
Cover design: Mark Laliberte
Interior design: Rafael Chimicatti
Guernica Editions Inc.
287 Templemead Drive, Hamilton, ON L8W 2W4
2250 Military Road, Tonawanda, N.Y. 14150-6000 U.S.A.
www.guernicaeditions.com

Distributors:
Independent Publishers Group (IPG)
600 North Pulaski Road, Chicago IL 60624
University of Toronto Press Distribution (UTP)
5201 Dufferin Street, Toronto (ON), Canada M3H 5T8
Gazelle Book Services
White Cross Mills, High Town, Lancaster LA1 4XS U.K.

First edition.
Printed in Canada.

Legal Deposit—First Quarter
Library of Congress Catalog Card Number: 2022947267
Library and Archives Canada Cataloguing in Publication
Title: Love is a place but you cannot live there / Jade Wallace.
Names: Wallace, Jade, author.
Series: First poets series (Toronto, Ont.) ; 23.
Description: Series statement: First poets series ; 23 | Poems.
Identifiers: Canadiana 20220435359 | ISBN 9781771837743 (softcover)
Classification: LCC PS8645.A45 L68 2023 | DDC C811/.6—dc23

For Ari

It seemed just beyond my reach, something
you could see through a window, but you
couldn't pass through. You could visit,
but you couldn't live there.

—Attributed to **Ann Bannon**

[T]he aim of psychogeography [i]s to see the urban
space in the light of desire rather than habit …
But it also implies a project to reform
or re-imagine the city.

—**Ian Buchanan**

Contents

VANISHING BEACH ◎◎◎

GENIUS LOCI ◎◎◎

◎◎◎ GHOST TRIP ◎◎◎

Shutter

In autumn, there is no apparent difference
between tourist towns and ghost towns.
Windows are shuttered, grit gathers on
porches, grass pushes at every crack.
A handful of trailers still run electricity
because some people can't afford another
home. But you and I know these towns
are not the same in any season.

In the tourist towns, we walk the sleepy
shore and watch lightning strike the
middle of the lake. You take a photo
of me surrounded by seagulls. I take
a photo of every store with a dirty name:
I Heart BJ's. Nut 'n' Fudge. Big Willy's.
When we pass other wanderers, we nod,
and leave each other to our solitude.

In the ghost towns, we don't stop the car.
We only drive, voyeuristic and slow, keeping
our camera in the backseat. Our eyelids click
like shutters to capture this road that has no
white lines, overhead wires, or street signs.
The leaves are so thick above us that we
can't see the colour of the sky. When we go,
we note a certain coldness in the wind,
let out breaths that we've been
superstitiously holding.

We'll never admit our preference for death.

Nothing Comes from Nowhere

There are numbers in your
hand that should tell us where
your grandfather is buried.
Section 28, you say.
I ask if you're sure;
beyond 14 is an empty field.
You shove the paper in your
back pocket and we spend the
next two hours reading every stone.
Some share your name, but none
of them are your grandfather.
We drive back and forth down
the adjoining road, fidgeting with
the map, looking for the rumoured
second half of the cemetery, but it
remains elusive as a cryptid.

You can't find your grandfather's
grave, like you can't be sure of
your grandmother's real name
because, even if you weren't
avoiding your father who tries
sometimes to kill you, there is
not one living member of your
estranged family who would admit
what kind of corners your grandmother
might have been forced into
or what became of her parents.

It must be unsettling for a trained
historian like you to be unable to
find the archive that can
show you your own bloodline.
You've consulted librarians
and miracle workers,
but your origins are still
as unknown as those of
the fingernail gouges you
found on the ceiling of
your bedroom one morning
after dreaming you were a raven.

Humans under Tganęnogahe

Above the sabkha, the plain
salt-crusted as seacoast, there is
lightning-white gypsum that shears
through shadowy dolomite.

The footpaths of miners run atop the stone,
winding outward and upward until they reach
a cluster of industrial buildings.
Roads sprawl from the heart of the
Hagersville mines like thoughtless limbs,
while the trees back slowly away.

Over the sleeping western shafts, six
Haudenosaunee nations share a five percent pittance
of the land they were promised by the double-
crossing British two centuries ago. A reward,
they were told, for their loyalty.

On the southern side is the town famous only
for the time it set ten million tires blazing.
For seventeen days—eternity by the metric
of TV news—firefighters fought to
quell the toxic smoke. Twenty-five
years later, it still grows inside them.

Cancer swells in their blood, their bladders,
their brains. In the hospital, the white
walls are made of gypsum and some
patients swear the tap water has the
dolorous taste of waste rock that finally
leached all the way to the lake.

The Innkeeper's Curse

In Delhi, Ontario, which could hardly be
less like Delhi, India, there is a woman who
runs a motel out of an office that adjoins her
family's apartment. While we're paying for
our room, one of her children comes in through
their door, carrying a dog-eared copy of
Around the World with the Word Gang, and
asks her mother to read to her.
Books abandoned on other nights form
colourful layers in the sediment of
invoices on the desk. The woman
hugs her daughter but goes on asking us
more questions than a Greek philosopher
about every city we've seen on our trip,
as if the turmeric we can smell simmering in
her kitchen has left her ravenous for a
world she can't go out to meet because
she has to wait for it to come to her in pieces of
international mail, in deliveries of Egyptian cotton,
in the bodies of globe-trotting travellers who
expect someone to keep the motel open
every day of the year.

Dead Reckoning

Wherever we are in southwestern Ontario,
Port Rowan is never that far away.
Always a reasonable drive
through farms
to the lake
on the edge of twilight.
But we struggle to arrive, no matter
how long we travel toward it or how
many times we stare incredulously
at the map, at road signs, at each other.

The first time we try seriously to find it,
we give up after five hours
and go home instead.

The second time, we resign ourselves to
inefficient wayfinding, managing the
half-hour drive in a mere four.
When we finally roll in, we walk the
empty Backus village in the dark.
Old farm machines loom over us,
with gears that look like they could grind bones.
No one yells at us to leave, though I start to wish
someone would. Just to reassure us it's possible.
By the time we get back to the car, our headlights
only deepen the shadows between the trees.

I turn to you and ask:
What lie is our map telling now?

You Have to Expect Fires

First it was a girls' school, then it was
a horror film set, and finally it was forsaken.
When a building is haunted by silence,
you have to expect that unexplained
fires will fill its cathedral arches
and bring it to collapse.

By the time we get there,
purple verbena is growing in
the hill of split bricks that remains.
I leave you staring at a chain-link fence
and cross a long stretch of pale, arid
rubble to a copse of trees reaching

their arms up out of the
ravine, whose slope glows
with chlorophyll and sunlight.
Rocks, half-buried in leaf litter,
are making arcane patterns
on the ground. Like crop circles,

like Nazca lines, like the seats and stage
of an outdoor theatre that fire
could not touch. No young spirits
wander but birds walk the earth
miming field mice and reciting
soliloquies for low-lying plants.

Maps of the Forest City

I

In London, Ontario,
World Serial Killer Capital '59-'84,
I go into a convenience store and ask if
they carry maps of London.
It doesn't have a map,
the clerk says,
and he probably means
the store doesn't stock the map,
but it sounds like cartographers
have foresworn the city.

II

Wellington Street is not
Wellington Road is not
Wellington Crescent
but they are all annexed
to each other.

I want to know why the city
can't come up with a new name.

You say, *Because they called
themselves London and they
christened their river Thames.*

III

Don't think you've found
a bank just because you see
a six-foot high sign
that says *BANK*.

IV

Down the street from the
all-night payday loan shop,
there's a hotel with
nouveau riche chandeliers
the size of small cars.

V

Where is the forest?
An "urban forest"
is not a forest.
An urban forest is a park.
An urban forest is a boulevard.
An urban forest is an insoluble paradox.

VI

London isn't wholly without wonder.
There's a bookstore,
which was once described as having
*cool things, especially on the top
and bottom floors,
but also on the middle floor.*
Three levels of cool, then.
A triple scoop ice cream cone.

There's an indoor market called,
of course, Covent Garden.
It's as old as 1845, good enough
for a theatre and an art school.
The market carries postcards,
fresh crêpes, living stones.
I'd buy a living stone
if I wanted a reminder
of how it felt to be here.

Impenetrable

By the time we reach Edgewater Beach,
the fog is so thick we could be anywhere on earth.
We see no shore, only the road under us heading south,
until we spy a sign for a fort. We've never heard
of it, but we stop because forts, by their nature,
must be haunted, even if they are now
surrounded by quaint suburban bungalows.

Fort Malden is known, when at all, for being
a place where Tecumseh and Brock
devised one whole strategy.
After it housed soldiers, it held
veterans on pensions. Later still,
it contained the overflow of so-called
'quiet chronics' from the Toronto asylum.
By the time we get to it, the only people
occupying the fort are a couple making out
next to the *No Swimming* sign and a
groundskeeper who does not approve
of the company. I try to remember
the last time I kissed you.

We do not stay long.
We leave the lovers to their fate
at the rubber-gloved hands of
the caretaker, who is in no danger
of leaving fingerprints
at a crime scene.

Cabbage Head

If a man walks out of his house, grim and
purposeful, carrying a large head of cabbage—

if a man refuses to look at you while you're
idling in his driveway—

if a man throws a large head of cabbage into
a cornfield with surprising fury—

       slide your gearshift into reverse,

       roll your tires slowly over the stones,

       and turn ninety degrees until you're
       back on a dirt road going anywhere else.

Don't try to catch the man's eye.

Don't ask why the chain holding the
Private Property sign is lying on
the ground under a tree.

No matter what the internet
told you about tours.

No matter how much you want to stand
on the bones of a homestead, calling
the names of a whole ruined family.

Skeleton Museum

The man acting like he's in charge calls it a museum,
but the only educational artifact I've seen
is a poster of the solar system, hanging on the
wall across from the toilet, which I noticed when
I was perched and scanning the room nervously.
In the facilities, spacious and sterile as a doctor's office,
I half-expected to find myself staring down the
beady eye of a hidden camera, or a stranger invading
through the inexplicable second door.

The man acting like he's in charge must be a con artist
or a thief. He's collected millions in semi-precious
gemstones and taxidermied animals, donated,
he claims, by dying friends and do-gooders.
But the non-profit corporate structure he describes
sounds more like a tax evasion scheme that lets him
spend his retirement glorifying himself to
people like you, who won't stop encouraging
him to talk, partly because you love a conspiracy, and
partly because he reminds you of your sharp father,
whom you can never see again, because
for twenty years he has wanted to
excise imagined sins from
your body with a knife.

The Lost Rooms

We drive eight hours a day,
scavenge French fries
and spaghetti from family
diners, then lock ourselves
in our motel rooms
and marvel at the nostalgia
of cable TV. At night,
our lives back home
are nothing more to us
than one of yesterday's reruns.
The world is only the strip
of highway that we can see
through the gap in the curtains.

Some nights, when I can't sleep,
I take bills out of my wallet
and spread them across a desk.
I don't count them;
I sit quietly
and resent every dollar
for being so small.
Money is the only hitch
that keeps us from disappearing.

◎◎◎ **NORTHERN EDGE** ◎◎◎

The Edge of Everything

We lived at the lonely edge of everything,
at the centre of nothing.

To the southwest was Downsview,
with its long flat stretches of green
attesting to its former life as a vast farm.
It had become a geographical identity crisis,
trying to hold its park next to its airport, on the
soil that used to house a Canadian Forces Base.
The former waiting ground for wars
had become a training ground for circuses.
A cynic might have asked
what the difference is.

To the east was Bathurst Manor,
the name implying an aristocracy that
didn't exist in either the neglected public
housing apartments or the apartments
that looked like neglected public housing.
The businesses were mostly restaurants
or closed. The restaurants were a
pastiche of international cuisines,
from the kosher dairy to the jerk joint
to the good Mexican restaurant named
Guacamole that only lasted a few months
and made me wonder if,
somewhere far south of there,
was a burger bar called Relish.

We lived at the place
where the subway ended.

On our northwest side, York University Heights
was home to the second largest school in
the country, a school that had,
nevertheless, been waiting decades
for the subway line to reach it.

Due south, the University of Toronto had
train tracks bordering it on three sides,
and we might have asked if we were not
old enough, or not good enough,
to have the same.

But we were used to the way that Toronto money
ran like a river to the lake.

Culture Gorge

Our neighbourhood had no art galleries,
though we had one house with a garden
of statues. Bright and unclothed,
the marbled bodies curled between
dark leaves in a shadow play of dance.

We had one bookstore,
where all the books were written
in a language few of us could speak.

We had cafés, yes,
but no one sat hunched in black,
scribbling over notebooks,
not even the teenagers.
Regulars watched a small TV
and looked like they missed the days
when they were permitted a
cigarette with their coffee.

Sometimes, bar band classic rock played
in the second-hand clothing shop.

We had a dollar store,
where the most expensive
thing you could buy
was closer to twenty dollars.
The store hosted a shelf of
ceramic figurines, one of which
was a frog, grinning through a
crooked jut of lipstick.

I wished it was a flaw made
by human hands,
so I could forgive it.

Rue

All families grieve when their children die;
     only rich families try to delegate their misery
to the public.

     For instance, there was a kid,
not even twenty years old,
     who met an early end when he
and his friends crashed their car on a rural Ontario road.

Spent with grief, his parents started a corporation
     and named it after him. All their unused tuition funds
would educate other people's children.

     Later, when his grandfather's real estate company
was building a luxury North York suburb,
     one of the roads was the inheritor of
the dead child's nominal legacy.

The charity dissolved but the road remained.
     We found it one day, between streets of houses
whose poorer owners had not yet
     been bought out. Seeing the unfamiliar name, you said,
He could be an activist! An astronaut!

You stopped a young couple, an old woman,
to ask if they knew who their street was named for.
    They didn't.

That night we traced the name to a textbook
    on grief and a study of the perils of college
fraternal life. I asked if it was cruel of me
    to be disappointed.

    No, you said. *What's cruel is making people
live in a graveyard.*

The Upper World

Living in a high-rise apartment,
our neighbours, when they existed to us at all,
were just single, hyperbolic traits.
It was like living in a stable full of allegorical horses.
We heard each other at night through the walls,
passed each other briefly in the hallways,
but never saw inside the stalls of our neighbours.

The horse who lived above us loved power tools.
Her drill ran eight hours on Saturday,
her hammer eight hours on Sunday,
her saw all through the week.
I never observed wood enter or leave the building.
Did her quarters grow closer nightly,
walls thickening with layers of screws and nails?
Was she a reclusive carpenter, smuggling small,
secret boxes of smaller, more secret boards
into her cloister to turn it into
a forest of her own design?

The two horses who lived down the hall were grandparents.
They pulled a chariot carrying two grandchildren,
who never seemed to grow older or taller,
from their apartment to the elevator and back again.
I never saw any of them out of doors.
They moved in a constrained but ceaseless ebb and flow,
a restless pacing that did not take them anywhere.

There were the horses who burned their dinner every night.
As dusk flickered across the day, the corridor alarm would
cry out again like it thought it caught the scent of a wolf.
But it was only ever the smell of horses,
eating grain that tasted of smoke.

In our apartment, we walked ovals around
the kitchen as the TV blared late into the night.
We struck notes on a glockenspiel
without ever reaching a melody.
The cat pled long and loud
for someone we couldn't see.
An angel, perhaps.

A Secret Park

When my friend from Ottawa came to visit,
I led us on a walk along the Don River, not
because I was convinced there would be anything
much to see, apart from an unused ski lift,
but because it seemed better than roaming the
aisles of the grocery store, or watching
football in a wordless dive bar.

We followed the edge of the water,
scampered our way up through
a labyrinth of steep, unmarked trails.
We were breaching a field that looked empty,
when we heard carnival music lilting over the hill.

Exchanging suspicious glances,
we climbed to the crest and found ourselves
unexpectedly surrounded by a crowd of families.
Children played lawless games of soccer,
parents cooked hot dogs on portable barbecues.
What is this? I asked. *Where are we?*

We passed through the crowd—and then
we were standing in a silver amphitheatre that
gleamed in the sun like a crashed UFO.

Beyond was another long stretch of field.
We crossed the grass and came out between
nondescript apartment buildings
on a street I'd never had reason to travel.
From that side, the secret park stretched
clear and wide for half a city block.

Human Geography

After three years of living in that apartment,
I still felt like we didn't belong to the
neighbourhoods it touched.
Our work and friends were elsewhere.
That place was for sleeping
and for buying groceries
and for leaving.
The glut of failing businesses suggested
other residents did the same.

There was one time, though,
when I felt myself almost a part of
that human geography we inhabited.
It was a mild evening in late summer.
The screen door to the balcony
was open for the cat.
I was in the bedroom,
which glowed pale blue like
a cloud preparing for rain.

Over the steady drone of airplanes and traffic,
the wind came in through the door
—a string joining tin cans—
and I could hear every proclamation made
in the transit station down the street.

◎◎◎ CYNIC'S GUIDEBOOK ◎◎◎

Everywhere Else

My boyfriend is bitter about New York City.
He says *It's the place people talk about*
instead of every other town on the continent.

I disdain all cities;
I prefer the spaces between them.
But my mother has wanted to go to

New York City for forty years
and I've never been cruel enough
to say no to my mother's dreams.

Now that I'm twenty-six, finally
settled in a job I can take a week off from,
my mother and I have made arrangements to travel.

I insist that we take the train
so that my mother can have the city
and I can have everywhere else.

Major Attractions at the Centre of the Universe

There is a place where you can stand and see
a large statue. It is at a distance, though.
If you pay money, and take a boat, you can
see the large statue from a slightly shorter distance.

There is ground where thousands of people died,
so they have built a memorial, which lovingly
throws thousands of litres of water into a dark pit.
They charge tourists money to go into an adjacent
building and hear about how the people died.

There is a place where the grass is so green
and the trees are thick with flowers.
Visitors can walk a concrete path and
look at the plants from a distance.

There is a corner so important that they stop traffic.
Tourists leave behind the trifling pop-ups of their tablets
to make a pilgrimage to this place where they can
marvel and take pictures of the biggest
advertisements of their lives.

There is a museum in the Empire City,
full of stolen artifacts. It is almost
as beautiful as it is troubling;
It is free, though, if you need it to be.

There is a very tall tower you can pay to ascend.
When you get to the top, you can look down
at the metropolis from far above and pretend
you are in an airplane, maybe,
hardly in the city at all.

Fun City

New York is a city of many opportunities—
to buy things, I quip. My mother is unimpressed.

In particular, it seems to me that certain New Yorkers
like to purchase cold-pressed juice and Tex-Mex food,
which they eat standing on the sidewalk.

Why does the land of the free
love to pay for things?

But Das Kapital der Welt also seems to like museums
and parks, which are often priceless, and would
probably be almost enough to make the city good,

if only it had
fewer people
fewer streets
less noise

and was generally completely different
apart from the free museums and parks.

The Importance of Choosing
Suitable Travelling Companions

Our hotel room is the size of a walk-in closet,
but is nevertheless comforting after a
day full of the clamour and aggressive
largeness of the Modern Gomorrah.

As my mother is turning out the light above
the top bunk on our second night in the city, she says,
There is no one I would rather be here with than you.
Which is nice of her, but only reasonable
when you consider the particular deficiencies
of her other friends and relatives.

So far, on our trip, I have treated all
food with deep suspicion and have only
ingested items that are both carbohydrates
and sealed in a bag prior to consumption.
My mother has, accordingly, resigned herself
to salads inhaled in the hurried intervals between
activities more important than basic sustenance.

I have done her the further disservice
of waking up early every morning,
preparing myself completely to go out,
then falling back to sleep for a full
two hours when she leaves for
ten minutes to shower.

Once we finally make it out of the hotel,
I slouch around the tourist attractions
making contemptuous noises.

I am also afraid of heights,
which is why my mother is
commenting on my
aptitude for travel as
she prepares to sleep in the top bunk
next to a chatty air conditioner.

On the other hand,
my mother cannot walk a full city block
without stopping to take a photograph,
a habit that, after the fiftieth block on any
given day, makes me almost feel like
we have earned each other.

Populations of Caput Mundi

I am nearly convinced,
after being here for two days,
that the City that Never Sleeps
is designed, and populated, by
robots, whose job is to give it
the appearance of being lived in,
so that tourists will not find
the empty monoliths unnerving,
but will instead continue to pay money
to see this odd city, which lacks
sufficient bathrooms, and places to sit,
and other things that robots might
plausibly forget that humans need.

The Five Boroughs

If you judge the prosperity of New York
by the number of people in it who are homeless,
then the city is in the midst of a second Great Depression.
How does New York keep them all from its tourist districts?

During our four days here, only three people asked us for change
and they all looked unusually alike.

And where does New York sequester its feral cats?
We haven't seen a single one wandering the neighbourhoods.

Toronto has known and roving bands of strays
that locals even arrange to feed.

Where does New York put all its aimless dreamers?
Its slow walkers?

Everyone in New York looks like they know
where they're going and they go there with great speed.
I feel a twinge of dystopian unease considering
what becomes of those who don't.

Taking the Greatest City in the World

To endure New York, you have to ignore yourself.
You have to walk to the tempo its streetlights set,
eat when its urban geography offers you food,
hear its cars and its calls and its twenty-four hour
construction as the white noise of a mind into which
you have been subsumed.

To love New York, I think, you would have to give
yourself up to it in awe, as though it were a god,
to set yourself adrift on its oceanic feeling.
Let yourself be consumed, digested like flotsam,
made into something the city can use.

I will vacate these streets the way I
dropped the Catholic faith ten years ago.

Fleeing the City of Neon and Chrome

When I first arrived, I wondered if
the best part of Gotham
would be leaving it.

And there was a pleasant languor
about waking up under a blanket of sunlight
as the train rolled smoothly north, catching
sight of the treed and sweeping Adirondacks
across the river.

Having been to New York,
I will go back to my own cosmopolis
with an unfamiliar sense that it is almost
quaint and calm. Reassuringly full of recycling bins.
I vow to never count myself a patriot, and yet,
something in America makes me
glad to call somewhere else home.

And so the best part of New York
was not leaving
but being gone.

Epistemology after the Big Apple

It's pretentious to think that
a person can know a city.
It's especially pretentious to think that
a person can know a city after four days.
No one can so quickly discern
each of the complex motions
of eight million people
and countless tourists
as they go over and under and
around and about each other.
Everything I know about this place
is necessarily glib.

In the end, we saw so little of the city.
We missed Harlem
and the Bronx
and Staten Island.
We spoke to almost no one,
bought almost nothing.
Without so much as a footprint
on a sidewalk
to mark our stay,
it's hard to be sure
we were there at all.

◎◎◎ VANISHING BEACH ◎◎◎

A Second Earth

For thirteen luckless, gaping months
I lived with my lover in rented condos
we had converted into monasteries.

Then you touched the
periphery of our sequestering
and the rain fell for forty days and

forty nights, flooding the cloisters.
All the widest brooms could not
sweep away the water.

Stranded on my bed, waves of
runoff licking the box spring, I tangled
my limbs into his like we were laver.

After, as I lay beside him,
the mattress was as small
as a clamshell.

I kissed his flushed cheek,
unsure of who I had betrayed,
but I felt like it was you.

When the water receded,
there was nothing to be done but
to leave the priory one by one.

Jolt

Before I ever kissed you,
before I ever touched the skin of your arm,
we walked westwards across the city,
following the day into the night.
At dinner, I met your friends,
shared a plate to have a reason
to lean close to you.

After ten hours together,
you walked me to the station.
As I rode off, I watched you turn
and head for home.
There was a pluck under my ribs
as though I'd gotten on the wrong train,
was not going the way I meant to.

I arrived at my apartment late that night
and my boyfriend's eyes ran the length
of my skirt asking why.
I smiled, displaced.
He said, *You can't keep
his cock out of your mouth for
ten minutes, can you?*

I didn't argue.
The truth was worse.

Rituals of Parsing

Breakups require rituals of parting.
After I told my lover I wanted
to be alone again, I tied seven
years of his straying hair
in a metre of silk. Binding
made them easy to carry,
and impossible to cry for.

But he wanted a mutual ceremony.
Feeling sorry, I swore I wouldn't
date anyone, wouldn't fuck anyone,
until he was gone. I kept
that promise, if keeping a
promise means finessing semantics,
weeks later, with someone else.

I think we can agree: it isn't
dating if the flowers I give you are
parrot lilies and yellow roses.
It isn't dating if the olives we order at the
bar are still not finished seven days later.
It isn't dating if we don't kiss in
the street before midnight.

And it isn't sex if there's a cloud
shifting between our bodies. It isn't
sex if the tide rises but never reaches town.

It isn't sex if I can't hear your neighbours,
can't see the sky, can't be sure that I am
not at home, asleep, dreaming,
in a bed where you have never been.

Mawkish & Tender

I was never sure I could be moved
by the mawkish, the tender,
but there is a persuasive
softness in you always
like the softness barely caught
by the corners of our lips
when you kiss me drunk and I
forget which of us was drinking.
I will come an hour and a half across
the city for that softness.
There is a softness in your eyes
when I am talking and it
never cuts me short.
There is a softness in your voice
when you say *gorgeous*.
A softness in your hand when I say,
You can spank me harder than that
and you do, but the difference
is the weight of a moth's wing.
There is a softness in all your foolish
offers of marriage that suggests you
might almost mean them if I say yes.
And your softness, I suspect,
is like the soft, faraway grass that wavers
beside your house upon the harbour.
There is a softness in you asking
if I would ever go there with you.
Hearing it, I know I can be moved—
the only uncertainty is distance.

Blood Shift

Since I arrived at your father's house on the coast yesterday,
I've spent several hours staring at the ocean, which,
if you believe the authors of certain beloved books,
is a favoured pastime of women about to
wade fully clothed into madness.
I don't think I'm a woman but I can't
tell the sea from the rain sometimes.
Of course I want to die
and of course I'm afraid of my body,
and other people, and nuclear arsenals,
and small trees, but I haven't yet
met anyone who could
convince me that they weren't.
Everything is dangerous
under the wrong circumstances.
That which doesn't kill you can still
humiliate you for years,
which is possibly a lot worse,
though I can't say for sure,
having probably never been dead.
How can I know that my heart never stopped
when I dreamt of falling off a pier
into a black lake? How can I know
that my heart did not restart, just
as quietly, before my awakening?
Sometimes I don't want to die,
I just want to be an incorporeal haze,
possessing the kind of sight that
does not require eyes.

Omniscience without responsibility.
I've tried, in this life, to reduce
myself to an eternal watcher.
I watch the waves, watch TV,
watch your family, who talk for hours
without requiring me to speak,
which is maybe why I like them,
and maybe why I like you,
who I can watch play guitar, watch sleep,
as if through the glass of a bell jar,
which is also maybe why I stayed
too long with my ex, who
was not a good listener
but loved an audience.
And then maybe I did not stay longer
because I would rather watch the ocean
than watch him, a little too much like
all those heroines who,
rather than swim in ennui,
prefer to sink into seawater.

Creatures that Were Not

Sprite

After a heavy fog, there is a second fog,
fragmented. Pearls of mist cling in cloudy
strings to all the formerly unseen spiderwebs
and the forest is suddenly full of sprites.

Puffin

A large bird is sitting on a rock that is half-
submerged in seawater. The bird looks like a
puffin, which makes no sense in this harbour.
I trip a bit on the beach shale as I'm hurrying
down to identify the bird, and it flies off at the
sound of clattering. It was probably a big duck.

Mammoth

The rocks uncovered at low tide are a
herd of woolly mammoths with their
backs to the cold. When I step on
their spines, thick hairs of seaweed
squelch and slip away in sheets,
threatening to take me with them.
I learn not to do it again.

Crow

According to your father, the five crows
of the harbour meet and converse at the
home of his neighbour who feeds them.
But I see the crows every time I walk
through the woods behind your
father's house and I swear
they're trying to talk to me.

The Way out of Paradise

At the party,
your uncle ribbed you about
bringing a new date home every holiday
and I became the unwilling evening,
watching for the night owl
on the way out of paradise.

The next morning, I go wading through
waist-high brambles and skidding down
long planes of shale to the pebbled beach.
Not knowing if I'll ever be back here again,
I'm looking for a piece to take home with me.

The first stone I consider is perfectly formed,
sheer white as the crinoline of the would-be
bride on last night's low-stakes local news.
She may never get to wear her dress because
of corporate bankruptcy and the perpetual
unpredictability of national postal services.

The next is smooth as sugar glass,
round as a green apple jellybean.
I put it down before I can lay it on
my tongue to see if it tastes sweet.

Another is magnificently split by
lightning, but too heavy to carry.

A fourth jumps out of my hand
when I try to hold it.

The fifth is a mountain on a map in
miniature, marked by topographical
lines I can't read.
I give it back to the water.

The sixth is as tiny and crooked as
a baby tooth. If I keep it I'll look
murderous. I'll be reminded of
your friend's mother, at the party,
who promised to persuade you to give
me a thousand babies. I could only shake
my head at her, alarmed. The garden is
not mine, but neither is the beach.

The stone I take is pure black,
as unrelentingly opaque as
birds' eyes in the night.
An enigma I need never answer.

Eavesdropping after Dark

Making the perilous walk to the beach at night
had only been an idle curiosity,
until you made me promise not to.
Hardly self-effacing or belligerent enough
to give in all the way to temptation,
I leave after you have fallen asleep
and walk just past the place where
the aureole of porch light ends.
I am hoping, at least, to hear the ocean.

After seconds of silence, I begin to make out
ship horns, water birds, and the endless whispers
exchanged between the waves and the stones—
rhythms not unlike the decades-long
conversation between the air and your lungs,
which I catch a few sentences of when I am
back inside, sitting at the kitchen table,
and you are still not yet awake.

The Ocean Is a Jeweller

I came here to be in love with you,
but I am caught up in awe of the sea.
I have even forgotten the waning white
light I used to worship in the dark.
My cheap running shoes are nearly worn
through from climbing down to the
beach every morning, afternoon, evening.
I am quick and clumsy and would
happily give myself up on these rocks,
rushing out to meet the ocean.

For all the sailors it has swallowed,
and all the ships turned to slivers,
and all the bottles split open on the rocks,
there is still a deceptive gentleness in the sea,
which smooths broken bones,
mellows splinters to driftwood,
sands broken shards into
a hundred ersatz jewels that
cannot cut even the tenderest foot.

I stand on the edge of the shore,
stretch out my hand, and the huge, shy
waves rise a little higher toward me
to lick at my fingers. My love is as
beautiful and deadly as the moon,
but so much closer.

Prevailing Currents

I'm not sure if it's because I was trying not to
have a panic attack at the time, but I was
unimpressed by Saint John's Reversing Falls.
My mother thought they should change the name,
you told me. *Because it looks more like the meeting
of two water flows that can't agree on which way to go.*
Or something like that. I was only half-listening.
Adrenaline is the loudest human hormone.
But whatever you and your mother before you
said sounded right, so I nodded.

The prevailing ambivalence of the Reversing Falls
has halted me all through the trip. In five days of
nothing much else to do, we've only had sex twice.
The second time we nearly stopped halfway through
for an argument. Not even for one of the handful of
conversations we should have had before leaving Toronto.
Here, amid all the emptiness of rural New Brunswick,
we still aren't filling anything in.

Vanishing Beach

At night, the water level rises and the
beach vanishes into the tide.
I stand on the overhanging cliff and
look for shadows of the lost
city under the waves.

In the morning, the water recedes
and I am given back all I ever missed.

For a while, I wished I could live in a small shed
on that ledge overlooking the shore.
But I want these rituals of returning,
fleeing and finding my way back,
to the waves and the tide and the stones,
through the mist gathering over and around us.

I like the way desire
takes the place of disappearance.

Nature Has Limited Patience
for the Human Condition

I think that growing old here
(in the smiling silence between
the ocean and the marshes, among
more crows than neighbours, with
no way out except by fallible car)
would only lead to swelling grief.

It is a treacherous crawl across the cliff face
to reach the rock I perch on to see the beach.
Twilight is growing like a cloud on my left knee,
which I have already, several times,
dashed carelessly against the stone.
One day, my joints would not withstand the slog.

But this week my cartilage is young
and does not yet mind.

Softcore

Softcore porn is my favourite kind of folk art.
On a Saturday afternoon, in an empty apartment,
while you are still a thousand miles away,
I fold and refold the edges of the bed sheets
in a pale imitation of origami,
turn out my feet until my knees are nearly
a dancer's parallel with the sky,
tilt the sun until it soft-soaps my skin.
When I am done, I find a glass bottle
thick enough to withstand an electric current,
compress a dozen photos inside it,
and float it out to you on the coast.

If I leave you,
or if the years turn me into a leaf
too dry and delicate to touch,
or if I die, I hope you will
paint all my plaintive hands
onto the kind of paper you can hold.

And if you leave me,
or if time clutters your veins
with all the relics of living,
or if you die, I hope you leave behind a vinyl record
that makes a needle moan, so I can teach a violin
to sling your pitches on another lonely
Saturday afternoon, while baseballs crack a
slow percussion on TV.

Too coarsely intimate for a garage sale
or a gift, we have no one but each other
to keep all this bright-eyed smut.
I hope we do. I hope it makes
at least one of us cry.

◎◎◎ GENIUS LOCI ◎◎◎

Sappho Détourné

You are homebound
and, with luck, in harbour now.
I am ready to give you back all
the dawning light scattered.
Do you bring me the bright
nightingale from the other
side of the sea? That bird is
a catastrophic god, a
black-winged dream that
we will need tonight, for
we shall have no sleep,
trembling like spring grass.
In the morning, and thereafter,
I will stay as long as you will
have me, for I cannot fathom
any woman who could meet
your grace or wisdom.
(May tempests take
him who can.)
If ever I go, I swear
I go unwillingly.

Heirloom Seeds

We moved into the rented lower half
of the house in spring. In the mornings, the walls
were dappled with the silhouettes of the scant
white carnations in the window box. It had
been a slow few years for the garden,
hardly humming with bumblebees, and
the plants were all struggling to make it
through the seasons.

But for the moment,
the flowers' fresh damp scent still spilled in the
kitchen window, so unlike the closed, moist
smell of the basement apartment we used to have.
We'd gotten lucky. Steady jobs took us out of
that gathering place for centipedes, who held
regular council in the cabinets, that drop point
for spiders who hid their secrets in crevices
under the floorboards, that dingy kingdom
where mould ruled us all in tyrannical silence.
Leaving was a kind of bitter triumph, because
it meant that someone else was moving in.

One afternoon, two weeks into our new lease,
I was cleaning out the back of the freezer and
pulled out a plastic bag with six tiny flax seeds.
When I looked closer, the seeds had legs:
the bag was a crypt for bugs, half a dozen of
them, perhaps kept by a former tenant who
wanted them identifiably whole.

That night when you got home, I led you
to the kitchen table to show you the corpses.
You put your face close to the counter
and shrieked. The bugs were moving.
They were slowly wriggling their
half-thawed limbs back to mobility.
Bedbugs bite, you breathed, remembering
the nursery rhyme your grandmother used
to sing, the nightmare you inherited.

We took our find into the backyard and
burned it, plastic bag and all, in a bonfire so
big that the neighbours came out to watch.
We let the flames blaze on, long after
the bugs had turned to ash, in a
superstitious effort to ward off
shadows from the past, always
trailing too close behind us.

Silvan

Crossing the bus station, in the
cooling light of six o'clock, amid
people leaving work and
careening into chaos, I am
suddenly overcome with
uncharacteristic tenderness.
A man, tall and shaggy as
a mountain covered in fir trees,
is watching his hands as he
cups the offering of a milky
ice cream cone so gently,
the way tree branches must
hold birds whose wings are
still too small for the sky.

Animals in Strange Houses

All down the lake edge,
a genealogy of trees had grown.
Generations of willow, maple, elm,
tangled their branches and breathed.

Developers followed a trail of paper
all down the lake edge.
They cut the trees up and carted them off
to disparate corners of the country.

Cottages rose up to take the forest's place,
with walls made of wood from the north.
Shingles of western cedar kept the floors dry when
storms swept east along the lake edge in the night.

The wild geese remained,
restless for several seasons.
They staggered the coast until the
growing flocks of children mostly

drove them from the beaches.
The geese tried to settle on narrow shores of
ponds, canals, and other small spaces that
human hands had made.

Four geese came to call a shopping mall
parking lot home. They lay with their sleek
heads curled like cats' into their bodies,
each to their own parking space.

They slept beside the cars
and garbage cans,
all in the places that
human hands had left them.

I Didn't Know It Would Grow to Be like This

I saw someone like you
at a bar in Novelty;
maybe it was you.
But I met you for real at
a flea market, when I was
meant to be getting neon signs,
shot glasses, magnets. I picked you
up as if by accident and took
you home with me instead.

After that, everything was
yes with you. *Is this okay?* I'd ask
and you'd say, *Yes, yes, yes.*
Once you'd given your affirmation to
my receding hairline, your validation to
my music choice, my voice, and my
disarrayed apartment, I wanted
you to stay and approve everything in
my life, every last quip and unwashed plate.
Confirm my suspicion that I'm worth something.
When you moved it was like you were
saying my name: *bob, bob, bob.*
We'd meet at baseball games or
antique stores and I'd take you home again
like it was the first time.

I swore I would keep you until
I died, but now that I am dying,
cancer in my bowels, my lungs, my liver,

I only want to send you out to see the world—
to meet my family, visit a museum,
join a travelling show. I will ask in dreams
if you are in a beautiful place and you will
smile and nod and I will know that the
world can still be good. Memories of me
will be brushed from your shoulder
and settle like dust wherever you go.

Signs in the Southern Hemisphere

Deception Island

The sea god breathes at low
tide, sends heat rising from the
black beach; a caldera is a
warm con that keeps back
the storms but not the ash,
which comes to cover all and
bury the whalers anew.
Penguins, unwitting,
attend the graves.

Paradise Bay

Big-eyed in the endless
light of summer, we
stayed the season in
the harbour until darkness
overtook our days.

Deep Lake

The voluminous blue of it
could turn the dead sea to
palest green; the shore is laid
with seal corpses embalmed
by a century of salt that
will not let the water be still.

Dry Valleys

Blood falls
but rain has not
since Earth's first
human footprint.
In their stone houses,
even bacteria hide from
the katabatic winds.

Fates Less than Death

Great Aunt Julie was an in-law and therefore doomed.
My grandfather and his seven siblings saw
each other into old age. They were septuagenarians
and all still alive. The firstborn sister had been living
with cancer for four years and just seemed a little tired.
Only the in-laws died. Only the in-laws succumbed.
All fates considered, Great Aunt Julie did all right.

She came into the family by marrying the second brother.
When she was in her middle years, she left one day without
a word. No one knew where or why she had gone.

Years later, her husband got a call from the motherland.
It was Julie, asking him to bring her back home.
He drove all the way to Quebec
and found her living with nuns.

From then on, Julie and her husband were only friends
who lived together. He helped her dye her hair
unconscionable colours. My grandfather once said
she looked like a widow-peaked werewolf child.

Sometimes, someone wanted to ask why
Julie disappeared all those years ago. But they didn't.
Her stories never made any sense anymore, anyways.

Inheritance

A plane crashed into
my grandmother's yard, so
she married the pilot.

By forty, she was
blind and had kidneys that
could not handle her blood.

The teenaged son she
could never relate to
flew to her on weekends.

Her husband's vessel became
trains; he traded air for earth, but
still held the sea in his glass.

My grandmother died young and
alone. People say I am like her, but
who knows if they mean clever or doomed.

Photographs, poetry she typed
while blind, a story in the news.
She is all paper now.

Ghost Feet

Like any apartment, yours eats socks,
but also swallows skirts and books.
Papers disappear and resurface eight months later.
Unfamiliar keys materialize out of nowhere,

not obviously associated with any door.
Inexplicable, unscientific appearances are commonplace
in the apartment where you've lived alone for years,
so there was no justification for shock.

Yet there you were, crouching in the shower one night,
beckoning me with one rubber-gloved hand,
whispering hysterically, *Do you see them?*
You wouldn't take your eyes off the bottom of the bath.

I walked over, stood beside you,
and saw the rough grey traces of heels and toes.
The tub was stained by a pair of human feet,
much smaller than mine.

We christened them *freaky baby ghost feet*
and went to sleep that night singing lullabies.

You Gather Their Bones

Even the feral cats don't touch this starling.
Her dark feathers are slick over her body puffed up
with the water of a spring thaw.
Her beak glows bone white,
a breathless ocarina outlasting its air.
She sleeps on a beach of bloated carpet,
black plastic, mud as thick as quicksand.

Behind her, the building walls are smooth and
pale as dunes and peopled with graffiti.
Caricatures of small dogs, ravens in dinner jackets,
and disembodied voices with edges dark as
ink preside over the starling's body. Nearby,
Styrofoam cups half-full with rainwater
and paper bowls holding aging cat food
sit untouched as the spread at a wake.
You and I stood a while with the
other accidental mourners.

For a moment, before we left,
you considered taking the starling home,
to a warm room lit by a soft sun slipping
through the leaves of old trees,
and laying her down there among the
fur and bones of the other unclaimed creatures
who came to you after their deaths.

Clairvoyance

There are people I love
because I was born to it,
people I love because we sighed through
years of school in adjacent desks,
small creatures I love because my
apartment is organized around them.
I love them because we keep our
memories alive in each other, because our
lines of time are knotted together and there is
no undoing them as we move forward and away.

But I love her differently.
I love her without perpendicular realities
that keep us coming across one other.
I could love her without the memory of
riffling through calendars of the moon,
looking for Christmas presents for our families,
love her without the memory of
holding her hand in a diner that looked
uncomfortably like the 1950's,
love her without ever having fallen
asleep in her boyfriend's bed.
I don't want to forget these things,
but I could,

and I would still want to know
her when we are old, quietly
missing our lovers who are gone,
while cats wind their way

around our mugs of bourbon and gin
and we cackle carelessly, turning each
other's long silver hair into
rainbows and braids.

The Mercy of Fairies

She smiled before she kissed me,
teeth flashing like talismans.
Misery left the room
and closed the door behind.
Her mouth tasted like meadowsweet, oak,
and broom, as though she were the incarnation
of the woman Math and Gwydion dreamed.

Her skin burned with vervain under my hands,
as her apartment rose farther above
the scent of night and cars and
road-worn courage below.
She took the cold lily from my brow
and adorned me in blood-red roses.
I want you now, she said.

Four words to finish the charm.
Still I did not linger in the circle of her room
when she suggested that I go.
I withdrew to the birds,
beginning to sing in the hedge,
and to the morning light inquiring
how many rings the world could hold.

Notes

The epigraph attributed to Ann Bannon is a quote that appeared in Natasha Frost's "The Lesbian Pulp Fiction That Saved Lives" (*Atlas Obscura*, 2018).

The Ian Buchanan epigraph is taken from *A Dictionary of Critical Theory (2nd Edition)* (Oxford University Press, 2018).

In "Humans under Tganęnogahe," Tganęnogahe is the Cayugan word for Hagersville, according to the *English-Cayuga/Cayuga-English Dictionary* (University of Toronto Press, 2014), compiled by: Frances Froman, who has taught the Cayuga language since 1978; Alfred J. Keye, who is a Faith Keeper and Cayuga language teacher; Lottie Keye, who had taught the Cayuga language for fifteen years as of the time of the book's printing; and Carrie Dyck, who is a linguist at Memorial University. This poem also relies on information supplied by the Six Nations of the Grand River's official website.

In "Maps of the Forest City," the bookstore referenced is City Lights Bookshop, and the person who described it to me as having "cool things, especially on the top and bottom floors, but also on the middle floor," was Gary Barwin.

I originally wrote the poems in *Northern Edge* for a collaborative suite co-authored with Terry Trowbridge.

The title "I Didn't Know It Would Grow to Be like This" is a quote from Bob Manak, the prodigious collector of bobbleheads about whom the poem is written.

"Inheritance" is for my grandmother, Nancy Fenderson, who really did all those things.

"You Gather Their Bones" is for Tristan Paylor and the cats of Kensington Market.

"The Mercy of Fairies" is a response to "La Belle Dame Sans Merci" by John Keats.

Acknowledgements

Thank you to the following presses and journals that published earlier versions of poems in this book, and their current or former editors:

- Anstruther Press and Jim Johnstone: *Rituals of Parsing* (chapbook): "You Have to Expect Fires"; "The Lost Rooms;" "Rue"; "A Second Earth"; "Rituals of Parsing"; "Animals in Strange Houses"; "Ghost Feet"; "The Mercy of Fairies"
- *Draft*, the publication of Draft Reading Series, and Maria Meindl: "The Edge of Everything"; "Culture Gorge"
- *Dusie* and Rob McLennan: "Silvan"
- *Feathertale* and Brett Popplewell: "Fates Less than Death"
- Gnashing Teeth Publishing: *Love Notes You'll Never Read* (anthology): "Clairvoyance"
- *Grain Magazine* and Alasdair Rees: "Sappho Détourné"
- *Held Magazine*: "Heirloom Seeds"
- *In/Words*: "The Mercy of Fairies"
- *Periodicities* and Rob McLennan: "Eavesdropping after Dark"; "Inheritance"
- *Quaranzine* and Third Estate Art: "Humans under Tganęnogahe"
- *Queer Out Here*, Allysse Riordan, and Jonathan Williams: "You Gather Their Bones"
- *Rock & Sling* and Laurie Lamon: "The Ocean Is a Jeweller"
- *Studies in Social Justice* and David Butz: "The Edge of Everything"; "The Upper World"; "Culture Gorge"; "A Secret Park"; "Human Geography"

- *The Nashwaak Review* and Stewart Donovan: "Animals in Strange Houses"
- *The Sandy River Review*: "I Didn't Know It Would Grow to Be like This"
- *Touch the Donkey* and Rob McLennan: "Everywhere Else"; "Fun City"; "The Population of Caput Mundi"; "Taking the Greatest City in the World"; "Fleeing the City of Neon and Chrome"; "Epistemology after the Big Apple"
- *untethered*, Stephanie McKechnie, and Nicole Haldoupis: "Softcore"
- *Where is the river: a poetry experiment* and Kiefer JD Logan: "Nature Has Limited Patience for the Human Condition"; "Signs in the Southern Hemisphere"; "Vanishing Beach"; "Creatures that Were Not"

This book was completed thanks to the generosity of the Ontario Arts Council and the City of Windsor's Arts, Culture and Heritage Fund.

This book was made possible by the Guernica Editions team, to whom I am grateful. The team includes Connie McParland and Michael Mirolla, publishers; Anna van Valkenburg, associate publisher; Elana Wolff, First Poets series editor; Dylan Curran, marketing assistant; and Rafael Chimicatti, interior designer.

This book was made better by my kind and thoughtful endorsers: Adam Dickinson, who has also been an encouraging and undogmatic mentor to me and to many; Annick MacAskill, who is an excellent poet but also an excellent critic; and Hollay Ghadery, who is an incredibly prolific reader and a friend to writers everywhere.

This book was enabled, shaped, and brightened by: my wonderful parents, Laurie Wallace, who taught me to read, and James Wallace, who taught me to pay attention to details; the ongoing moral and artistic support of Mark Laliberte, who is not only my steadfast significant other but is also the world's greatest cover designer; the submission and editing support of my kindred spirit, Kamila Rina; the intellectual support and travelling company of the inimitable Terry Trowbridge; Petre Lozinov, James Millhaven, and Jeremy Colangelo, who have been longtime friends and sometimes readers and editors of my work; Rahat Kurd, whose writing I admire and who read this book and made me think twice about it; Maria Meindl, an extraordinary community builder, who always makes me feel welcome; Priscilla Brett and Jordan Fry of Grey Borders Books, and Jim Johnstone, of Anstruther Press, who put out my chapbooks when I was especially flailing and new to all this; the once-constant company of my dear adopted cat Ari (c. 2010-2021); and the luminous existences of numerous other people and beings.

About the Author

JADE WALLACE is a writer from the Niagara fruit belt, currently living just south of the Detroit River and just north of Lake Erie. Wallace's writing has won the Muriel's Journey Poetry Prize and *Coastal Shelf*'s Funny & Poignant Poetry Contest, placed third in the Ken Belford Poetry Contest, been a finalist for the Wergle Flomp Humour Poetry Prize, and been nominated for The Journey Prize. They are the author of several solo and collaborative chapbooks, the reviews editor for *CAROUSEL Magazine,* and the co-founder of MA|DE, a collaborative writing entity. *Love Is A Place But You Cannot Live There* is their first book. Stay in touch: jadewallace.ca

MIX
Paper
FSC® C100212
www.fsc.org

Printed in January 2023
by Gauvin Press,
Gatineau, Québec